TERRIFIC TRAINS

KINGFISHER
LONDON & NEW YORK

Text copyright © Tony Mitton 1998
Illustrations copyright © Ant Parker 1998

Published in the United States by Kingfisher, 175 Fifth Avenue, New York, NY 10010
Kingfisher is an imprint of Pan Macmillan, London.

Distributed in the U.S. and Canada by Macmillan, 175 Fifth Avenue, New York, NY 10010

Library of Congress Cataloging-in-Publication Data
Parker, Ant.
Terrific trains/Ant Parker, Tony Mitton.— 1st ed.
p. cm.
Summary: Rhyming text introduces a variety of trains as they leave a station, rush along the tracks,
and arrive at the platform where travelers are waiting.
1. Railroads—Juvenile literature.   [1. Railroads.]   I. Mitton,
Tony. II. Title.
TP148.P37   1998
625.1—dc21   97-39703   CIP AC

ISBN 978-0-7534-5306-3

Kingfisher books are available for special promotions and premiums.
For details contact: Special Markets Department, Macmillan,
175 Fifth Avenue, New York, NY 10010

For more information, please visit
www.kingfisherbooks.com

Printed in China
10 9
0215

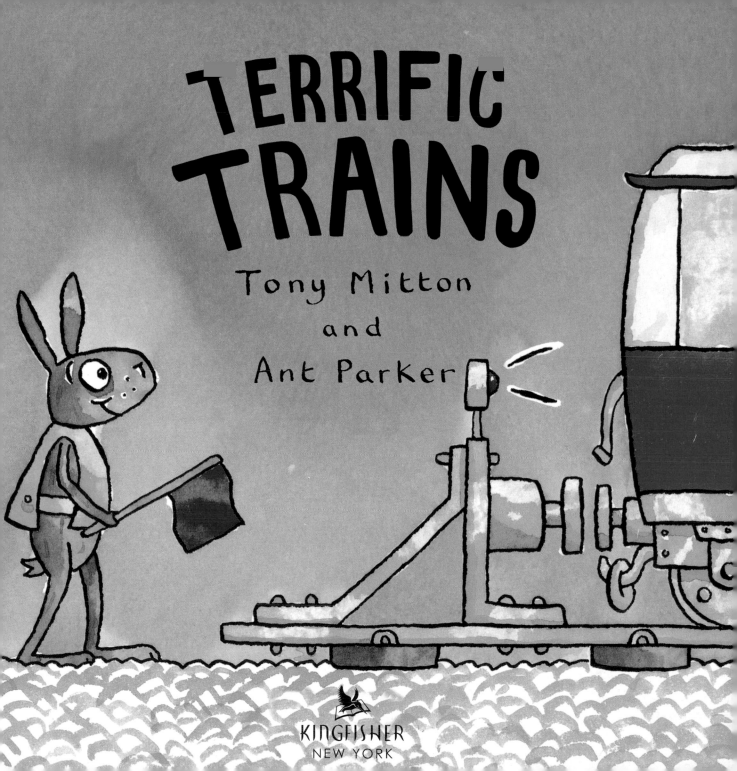

TERRIFIC TRAINS

Tony Mitton
and
Ant Parker

KINGFISHER
NEW YORK

Big trains, small trains, old trains and new,

rattling and whistling—Choo, Choo, Choo!

Starting from the station with a whistle and a hiss

steam trains huffing and puffing like this.

Diesel trains rushing as they rattle down the line,

varning us they're coming with a long, low whine.

Metal wheels whirl as they whizz along the track.
They shimmer and they swish
with a slick click-clack.

Coaches are coupled in a neat, long chain.
An engine pulls the coaches,
and that makes a train.

If a train meets a river or a valley or a ridge,

the coaches rumble over on a big, strong bridge.

If a train meets a mountain it doesn't have to stop

It travels through a tunnel and your ears go pop!

When too many trains try to share the same track,

he signals and the switches have to hold some back.

When the rail meets a road,
there's a crossing with a gate.

The train rushes through
while the traffic has to wait.

Trains travel anytime, even very late.

This train's delivering a big load of freight.

This train's for passengers.
It's ready at the station.

All aboard and wave goodbye—
we're going on vacation!

Train parts

rails

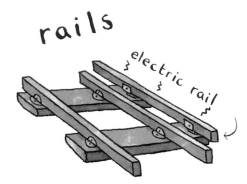

electric rail

these are metal strips that form a pathway called a **track** or **railroad line**. Some trains get their power from an electric rail

whistle

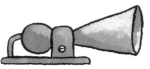

this makes a noise to warn everyone that the train is coming

Freight car

this is for carrying goods, called **freight**

signal

this tells engineers when to stop and go

coach

this is for carrying people, called **passengers**

switches

these are the short rails that move to let a train switch from one track to another